Learn How to Enhance Your Career and Employability Skills

# ACCOUNTING

## GET HIRED WITHOUT WORK EXPERIENCE

## AWARD WINNING AUTHOR

### MAYOORAN SENTHILMANI
ACMA, CGMA, MSc, BSc

D1430525

ISBN: 978-0992869410
ISBN-13: 0992869412

# CONTENTS

# ACKNOWLEDGMENTS

I would like to express my deepest appreciation to my mentor Raymond Aaron, the New York Time Best Selling Author, who conveyed a spirit of adventure in regard to writing books. Without his guidance this book would not have been possible.

My sincere thanks go to the people who gave me assistance throughout this book; to all those who provided support, offered feedback, and assisted in the editing, proofreading and design.

I would like to thank DVG STAR Publishing for supporting me to publish this book.

This book would not have been possible without the support and encouragement of my lovely wife, Labosshy Mayooran.

Last but not least, I would like to thank my parents and teachers for guiding and mentoring me throughout my childhood to become an expert in my professional life, and the success of the book is dedicated to them.

# GET HIRED WITHOUT WORK EXPERIENCE

## CHAPTER 1

# GETTING STARTED

## What is accounting?

Accounting is the systematic process of recording, reporting and analysing the financial transactions of a business. In simple terms accounting helps a firm to identify whether the business is profitable or not.

The accountant who is responsible for maintaining the accounts of the company is expected to follow accounting principles and standards such as generally accepted accounting practices, also known as GAAP.

## Which accounting is for you?

There are several types of accounting practiced in the corporate world, including financial accounting, management accounting, governmental accounting, tax accounting, forensic accounting, project accounting, and social accounting.

**Financial accounting**: The process of producing financial statements for external use. The financial statements will include the past and present performance of the business following certain accounting standards known as GAAP. There are many accounting systems available to prepare financial accounting, for example: sage line 50, QuickBooks and SAP.

**Management accounting**: Prepared for the internal use of the company. This takes place in the form of budgeting, cost accounting and so on. This is where management needs to be placed at higher priority as this will highlight the key performance indicators of the company, for example: sales, labour cost and food cost.

## Accounting: how it works

The concept of accounting starts with the ideology of double entry. In simple terms, double entry means each and every transaction has a debit and credit effect. Given that the revenue is equal to the expenses of the company we can arrive at the fundamental formula of double entry.

$$\text{Assets} = \text{Liabilities} + \text{Equity}$$

For example if we take cash sales, the double entry for this will be as follows;

Cash – debit

Sales – credit

As the cash is coming in to the business it is debited and the sales are credited. We follow a standard practice for double entry which will communicate which entry should be debited and credited.

|  | Debit | Credit |
|---|---|---|
| **Asset** | Increase | Decrease |
| **Liability** | Decrease | Increase |
| **Income** | Decrease | Increase |
| **Expense** | Increase | Decrease |
| **Shareholders' Equity** | Decrease | Increase |

The table above provides a clear picture about the basic double entry techniques used in accounting. Now let's look at some of the basic definitions of accounting terms used in accounting practices:

**Asset** – Any item of economic value owned by the company. For example: land, furniture, property, and so on. Assets can be mainly classified as long term assets, current assets (short term), and intangible assets (goodwill of the business).

**Liability** – It is an obligation a company needs to pay. It can be in the form of debt or suppliers payments. Liabilities can be classified as current liabilities, which are the debt which needs to be settled within one year, and long term liabilities which are the debt which needs to be settled over a longer period (more than one year).

**Income** – The total amount of money generated by the company for goods sold and services provided during a certain time period.

**Expenses** – Any cost of running the business.

**Shareholders' equity** – An ownership stake in the company in the form of common stocks or preferred stock. It can also be calculated by deducting total liabilities from the total assets of the company.

## Financial statement: what does it include?

**Income statement** – Accounting of revenue, expenses, and net profit for a certain period. The period can be on a quarterly or yearly basis. The income statement is based on the fundamental equation,

**Income = Revenue – Expenses**

Income statements will help you to identify whether the profits margin the business is generating is in line with industry standards.

**Balance sheet** – Indicates the financial condition of a company at a specific time period. The first part of the balance sheet includes the assets a company owns and the second part includes the source of financing.

**Cash flow statements** – Enable the management and investors to understand where cash is coming from and where the cash has been spent.

## Which business structure is for you?

When you are structuring your business it is very important to select the correct business structure, as it is going to affect the amount of tax you are going to pay and the paper work you have to do.

The most common forms of businesses are:

- Sole proprietorship
- Partnership
- Corporation
- Limited Liability Company (LLC)

## Sole Proprietorship

If you intend to work on your own, this structure will best suit your needs. Under sole proprietorship the owner is responsible for the debt. The business structure is very simple and easy to set up.

The external source of financing will be very difficult for sole proprietorship. In these instances the owner has to rely on his savings or investments.

## Partnership

If you intend to operate with several business partners, then a partnership is the structure you must choose. A partnership can be classified by two types:

- General partnership
- Limited partnership

**General partnership** is where several partners manage the business and take responsibility for the business obligations.

**Limited partnership** involves both the general and limited partners. The general partner's role will be similar to the general partnership. On the other hand, limited partners serve as investors only. They will not have any ownership stake in the company.

The main benefit of a limited partnership is tax savings; you don't need to pay tax on your income. You can pass it on to the profit or loss you made during the period.

On the negative side, general partners are responsible for business obligations. In addition, it is more expensive to set up than sole proprietorship, as it requires more legal and accounting services.

## Corporation

A corporation is an independent legal entity, and it is very complex and difficult to set up. However the benefit which arises from this model is you are not responsible for the business obligations, so your personal assets are not at risk.

Another plus is the availability of financing: the corporation can issue stocks to raise funds. It can be in the form of common stocks or preferred stocks.

The downside of a corporation is the cost involved with preparing accounting and tax returns. As the business structure is more complex you need the advice from an attorney as well.

Another drawback of a corporation structure is you may need to pay double tax. The corporation should pay the corporation tax applicable to them. The second form of tax comes with dividends. One possible way to overcome this double taxation is to increase the compensation for the partners. But it is very important to study the maximum compensation allowed in accounting standards for business partners.

## Limited Liability Company

A Limited Liability Company (LLC) is a hybrid company which brings in the features of both a partnership and a corporation. The partners are not responsible for the business obligations, and it avoids the double taxation.

An LLC doesn't have any limitations on the number of shareholders a company can have. Furthermore, the shareholders can be involved in the business practices.

You should always keep in mind that when you are using a LLC structure you should use an experienced accountant who has sound knowledge in several accounting practices.

## Government bodies, registering and filing

## Registering your business with companies house

When you are planning to register your business you must have the following information with you:

**Company Name and Address** – It is a rule of thumb that you cannot use an existing business name. You can always check the availability of the name in the company registration web portal. If the name already exists you have to find an alternative name for your business.

**Officer Details (Director and Secretary)** – To set up a private limited company you should have at least one director who is over 16 years old. You can also have a secretary for your entity but it is not mandatory. You should have the following information before registering the name of directors and secretaries:

- **Full name**

- **Residential address** - This can be the registered address. The address should also mention the state or country where the address is situated.

- **Nationality, occupation, date of birth and any former names** (that have been used for business purposes in the last 20 years).

- **'Consent to act' information** - In order to meet the signature requirement you may need to provide any 3 of the following:

  - Last three digits of your telephone number

  - Last three digits of your National Insurance number

  - Last three digits of your passport number

  - Your mother's maiden name

  - Your eye colour

  - Father's first name

**Share Capital and Shareholder Details** – You must submit the name and address of the shareholders of your entity. Furthermore you should also mention the amount of shareholdings owned by the shareholders.

**Payment** – You can make payment via debit card or credit card after setting up an online account.

## Starting a Company or Organisation and Corporation Tax with regulations

When you are registering your entity it is very important to communicate the existence of your entity to revenue and customs for tax purposes and other legal matters. This guide explains what you need to do and when.

## New companies and organisations and Corporation Tax

When you set up a new company or organisation that's liable for Corporation Tax

- You must communicate your business existence within a certain time period, for example, within 3 months.

- You must pay your tax obligations on time
- You must file your tax return on time

When you are registering your company with revenue and customs, they will use the information you have provided to set up a computer record for your entity. Then they will create a unique reference number, known as a UTR (unique tax payer reference number).

They then send a form called Corporation Tax Information for New Companies to your company's registered office. The form will also include your

14

UTR, so please keep that reference number in a safe place. You need it when you are contacting revenue and customs in relation to a tax query.

## Using revenue and customs online services

**If you used the revenue and customs online service** your company will be automatically enrolled for corporate taxation online and then revenue and customs will post you the pin within seven days.

It is very important that you keep that pin very safe. You should validate the pin within short time span.

## Using an accountant or tax adviser to deal with revenue and customs

You can appoint an accountant or tax adviser known to revenue and customs as an agent to deal with revenue and customs on your behalf. The agent will communicate the tax position of your company on your behalf.

## Record keeping for Corporation Tax

If your company or organisation is liable for Corporation Tax, you must keep and retain adequate business and accounting records to file an accurate Company Tax Return and calculate how much Corporation Tax you need to pay.

## CHAPTER 2

# MONEY MATTERS

Every new business needs money during the starting-up process. This is to buy equipment, establish the office, to pay the bills, for marketing and so on. This is all before the first sale is made.

You have to choose the right financing option in the first place, and to do so you have to evaluate the advantages and disadvantages of the available financing options. This book will help you to analyse and choose the best options available to you according to your specific needs and circumstances.

In order to work out your financial requirements, you have to prepare a business plan. This business plan should include information about your business operation and essential financial forecasts. A good business plan will help you to convince your bank or other potential sources of finance that you know what you are doing and their money will be safe with less risk.

You must have an accurate idea of your financial

requirements, as your customers may not pay you immediately. It's better to prepare a weekly cash flow forecast for the next 6 months.

Financing options available to you during the start-up period

1. **Use your own money**
   You can consider doing a re-mortgage, or using a credit card or unsecured personal loan, or selling assets, etc.

   **Advantages**

   - You will have more control, as there is no need to give any return or any shares to others
   - No need to worry about outside investors withdrawing their support at any time

   **Disadvantages**

   - Possibilities of losing your home or assets in case your business fails
   - Puts pressure on you and your family

2. **Family and friends**
   You have to consider the worst case scenario of losing their money if your business fails.

**Advantages**

- May offer easy terms, such as interest free

**Disadvantages**
- Pressure on you and your relationship with them

3. **Borrow from banks by creating a credible business plan**

   **Advantage**

   - You can match the term of a loan to your requirements
   - Less family pressure

   **Disadvantage**

   - The need to do a regular payment might cause cash flow problems
   - You may have to offer some security

## 4. Outside investors to finance your business

You could issue ordinary shares to investors in return for their capital.

### Advantages

- Bring additional expertise and funding
- No need to pay until you can afford to pay

### Disadvantages

- You may have to share your business and profits
- Investors may want control over how you manage the business

## Possible sources of finance available to you after the start-up period

**Retained profits**: This is the net earnings which arise after you pay the tax. During the initial stage of the company's life cycle it is rare you will be paying dividends. The company only focuses on business expansion and rapid growth. These retained earnings can be kept for future investment. It is a very useful technique to fund business expansion.

**Bank overdraft:** This will be provided by the bank, and it depends on your credit rating. If you are a start-up company , the amount you can borrow may be limited. Overdraft is a very useful technique for short term cash flow issues, such as making payments to suppliers. It should be noted that it comes with an interest cost.

**Trade Credit:** This approach is a very useful technique. Trade credit means you are delaying the payment to your suppliers. Once again it depends heavily on your bargaining power. If your bargaining power is high then you can demand a higher credit period. On the other hand if your bargaining power is low you may need to make a payment immediately. To use this technique in an effective and efficient way you have to build relationships and enhance the trust between you and suppliers.

**Hire purchase:** This approach is where you make an initial down payment and make the rest of the payment as equal instalments. You have to bear the interest cost. At the end of the hire purchase period the assets belongs to you.

**Leasing:** This approach is similar to the hire purchase. The only difference is at the end of the leasing period the asset doesn't belong to you. This technique can be used when you don't want to own the assets.

**Long term Bank loan:** Borrowing options from the bank can be a fixed interest loan or variable interest loan. When you are borrowing you should make sure whether your business is generating sufficient cash flow to make loan repayments. You need to provide collateral to borrow the money.

**Issue of additional share:** Shares can be issued to attract more capital to the business. The issue with this approach is the ownership of your business will be diluted and the new investors might have a different view about the business.

## Why use a business bank account?

When you register the company, next important step to follow is open a separate business bank account. This is to distinguish your personal bank account from your business bank account. The cash inflow and outflow should be carried out using the business bank account.

This systematic approach not only will allow you to have an accurate tracking system but will also be very useful during tax filling and audit periods.

When you are opening your business account please check for the following features

- company debit card
- company credit card
- overdraft and loan facilities
- asset finance
- commercial mortgage

## Collecting money from your customers

If you are a service provider or selling goods to your customers you need to invoice the customers. If you are registered for Value Added Tax (VAT) then you can claim VAT in your invoice. If not, you cannot claim the VAT.

As a business you might have one-off customers and long term customers. With one-off customers you don't need to build the relationship, as you will collect your payments immediately. The issues arise with the long term customers who have the potential to buy your services or goods on a continuous basis.

The customers will ask for extended credit periods. You may be forced to agree with their credit terms if your business depends heavily on their buying power. The delay in their payments can create cash flow issues for you.

Here are some things to remember when calling past-due customers:

**Understand the negotiation process** – Negotiation involves the skills you have developed as the business owner. If you have a better understanding with each other, then there won't be any issues in your relationship.

**Focus on a win-win solution** – Create a win - win solution for both parties. Listen to your customers and understand their cash flow problems, but you should also put a credit limit on each customer. This can be made based on their earnings potential.

**Be patient and confident** – Most of the time the common mistake all of us make is to demand for an immediate payment. It can ruin the entire relationship you have built. So it is also important to develop your patience skills and to be confident about your customers.

## CHAPTER 3

# CONTROL YOUR COST

### Keeping track of business cost

Keeping track of your business cost is very important. If you don't have a proper tracking method you may have the wrong picture about your business model. At the end it is all about the net cash flow your business is generating.

Business incurs several costs including production cost, labour cost, administrative cost, and distribution cost and so on. When you record all these costs it will give a clear picture of where your money is going out.

You can use accounting software or systems such as sage accounts or QuickBooks to record your income and expenses.

When evaluating the business, performance management accounting comes into play. You can prepare the basic management accounting in an excel sheet. Forget about the model, just enter the cash inflow and cash outflow your business incurs during the year on a regular basis.

Then do a variance analysis using the previous year's data. For larger variances conduct an investigation. Find out solutions to reduce the cost.

**For example** last year your labour cost was £60,000 and this year it has increased to £80,000. The variance is £20,000. There can be several reasons for that increase. It may be due to additional shifts. To find out whether the additional shifts have increased your revenue will give a clear picture about that cost.

## Cash is the king

A business cannot survive without cash inflow in the long run. This is where you should always prepare cash flow statements. This approach identifies whether your business is generating sufficient cash to manage your expenses.

The cash conversion cycle is also key in running a business. The cash conversion cycle can be calculated as follows:

$$CCC = \text{receivable days} + \text{payable days} - \text{inventory days}$$

# Sample Cash Flow Forecast

| Week Ending | 05/01/2014 | 12/01/2014 | 19/01/2014 | 26/01/2014 |
|---|---|---|---|---|
| Opening Balance | 100,000 | 91,000 | 96,500 | 103,000 |
| **Bank- TO CREDIT** | | | | |
| Expected Sales | 12,000 | 10,000 | 14,000 | 10,000 |
| Net cash inflow | 112,000 | 101,000 | 110,500 | 113,000 |
| Unpresented Chq | 1,500 | | | |
| Direct debits | 1,000 | 2,000 | 1,000 | 500 |
| Rent | 5,000 | | | |
| Business Rates | 1,000 | | | |
| Wages | 5,000 | | | |
| Loan Repayments | 5,000 | | | |
| Corporations Tax | | | | 1,000 |
| PAYE | | | 4,000 | |
| VAT | | | | 10,000 |
| Cheque run | 2,500 | 2,500 | 2,500 | 2,500 |
| Total Expenses | 21,000 | 4,500 | 7,500 | 14,000 |
| **Expected Closing Bank Balance** | **91,000** | **96,500** | **103,000** | **99,000** |

You should also prepare cash flow projections, which you can prepare in an excel sheet. Project the sales income as per the last year, then identify the cost which will be debited from your bank account. This can includes direct debit such as electricity, rents, business rates, and supplier payments.

This approach will enable you to manage cash flow issues. Planning in advance always helps for a rainy day.

## Budgeting

Budgeting is where you prepare your financial projections for next year using this year's data. Using budgeting, you can set targets for your departments or branches. Setting performance related tasks are always a confident boost for store managers and staff.

## Sample Forecasted budget

| FORECASTED SALES 2014-15 | 520,000 |
|---|---|
| | |
| Cost of Sales | 156,000 |
| Cost of Sales % | 30.00% |
| | |
| Labour | 130,000 |
| **Labour %** | **25.00%** |
| | |
| **Total Direct Cost** | **286,000** |
| **Gross profit** | **234,000** |
| **Gross profit Margin %** | **45.00%** |
| | |
| **Expenses** | |
| Rent | 40,000 |
| Service charges | 5,000 |
| Water | 2,000 |
| Rates | 2,000 |
| Insurance | 1,000 |
| Electricity | 10,000 |
| Security charges | 8,000 |
| Postage & stationery | 2,000 |
| Telephone | 4,000 |
| Advertising | 2,500 |
| IT | 3,000 |
| Repairs & maintanance | 10,000 |
| Cleaning | 10,000 |
| Clothing | 1,000 |
| Total Expenses | 100,500 |
| | |
| **Operating profit** | **133,500** |
| **Operating profit %** | **25.67%** |

CHAPTER 4

# KNOW YOUR KEY PERFORMANCE INDICATORS (KPIs)

You should be able to identify the right KPIs for any business. You have to define the strategy first and then closely link your KPIs to the objectives. This would help you to track performance and navigate your way to success and growth. Few examples are as follows.

**To measure and understand your financial performance**

1. Net Profit Margin

2. Gross Profit Margin

3. Operating Profit Margin

4. EBITDA

5. Sales Growth Rate

6. Return on Investment

7. Debt-to-Equity Ratio

8. Cash Conversion Cycle

9. Working Capital Ratio

10. Price Earnings Ratio

**To Measure and understand your customers**

1. How likely is it that a customer will recommend your business to a friend?

2. How much profit do individual customers bring to your business, after deducting the costs of attracting and keeping them happy with advertising, customer services etc?

3. How many of your customers are going to come back again for repeat purchase? How loyal they are to your brand, organization or service?

4. How well do you translate enquiries, sales calls and web page views into paying customers?

**To measure and understand your internal processes**

1. Are you using your resources fully?

2. Are your projects reaching completion before deadline?

3. Are your projects reaching completion within budget?

## To measure and understand your employees

1. How much is unauthorized staff absence costing your business?

2. The financial value added to the business by individual members of staff.

3. How staff rate each other as well as themselves

**CHAPTER 5**

# THE BASIC TAX FOR YOUR BUSINESS

**What is VAT?**

VAT is a tax charged when a VAT registered company is selling products and services to their customers. On the other hand the VAT registered company can claim VAT for the products and services they have paid.

There are three rates of VAT:

- Standard
- Reduced
- Zero

There are also some goods and services that are

exempt from VAT.

In order to register yourself for VAT purposes, you have to be in a business which is generating income on a continuous basis. One-off income will not qualify you for VAT registration purposes.

## When you must register for VAT?

If you're in a business which is selling products and services which can be taxed, then you should register yourself with Revenues & Customs for claiming VAT.

For example, in the UK you can register yourself with Revenues & Customs if you meet the following criteria:

- Your Business turnover exceeded £82,000 last year.
- You estimate that the turnover will exceed the £82,000 limit very soon.

## How VAT is charged and accounted for?

The VAT you claim from your selling goods and services is called output tax, and the VAT you pay on the purchase of goods and services is called input tax.

## Filling in your VAT Return

If you are registered for VAT then you must file your VAT return on a timely basis, generally known as quarterly basis. The VAT return should include the output tax, input tax and the net tax.

If the output tax is higher than the input tax, you have to make the net payment to Revenues & Customs. This can be a direct debit or BACS payment. On the other hand if the input tax is higher than the output tax, you can claim the net from the Revenues & Customs.

## Exempt items

There are few items which are not covered by VAT. A few examples are:

- Insurance
- Providing credit
- Education and training, if certain conditions are met
- Charity fundraising
- Services provided by doctors and nurses.

## Corporate Tax

## What is Corporation Tax?

Corporation tax is a tax charged on the net taxable income of companies.

Taxable profits for Corporation Tax include:

- Trading profit
- Capital gains
- Investment profit, not the dividend

## What is an accounting period for Corporation Tax?

Generally it is considered to be a 12 month period. It is very important to note that you cannot choose your tax period.

## Do you need Tax Adviser?

You can directly deal with Revenues & Customs in relation to tax purposes, or you can assign a tax adviser. You can save a lot of money by implementing tax planning and using good tax advice. A **virtual tax adviser** will be a great value addition for your business with a very affordable cost.

If you need more advice on filing your company tax return and paying tax, please contact your local Revenues & Customs. They will be happy to help you.

## CHAPTER 6

# HOW TO ANALYSE PERFORMANCE

## How to use ratio analysis to identify financial performance

Ratio analysis is a key tool in analysing the financial statements of a company. As financial statements represent past and present data, it can be very complex for a reader to understand. With the use of ratio analysis, a reader or investor will be able to understand the financial performance of a company.

Below are some of the key financial ratios which can be used for financial analysis of a company.

## Profitability ratios

Profitability ratios can be used to measure the ability of the company to generate profitability. The profitability ratios can be compared with the historical figures or with peer companies to identify its current position. Under this we are going to discuss two profit margins: gross profit margin and net profit margin.

## Gross profit margin

You can calculate the gross profit margin as follows:

### Gross profit margin = Gross profit/ Net sales

Gross profit can be calculated by deducting the cost of sales from net sales. Generally the cost of sales includes raw material cost, labour cost and manufacturing cost.

This ratio measures the ability of the management to efficiently reduce the cost of sales. A higher ratio is considered to be a more favourable one for the business.

## Net profit margin

You can calculate the net profit margin as follows:

### Net profit margin = Net income/ Net sales

This is the bottom line profit. Net income can be calculated by adding other incomes from gross profit and by subtracting other expenses from the total gross income.

This formula measures the ability of management to control administrative expenses, distribution expenses and other expenses.

For example, a company is making a sufficient gross profit margin but the net profit margin is negative. The reason for this is a higher finance cost.

By comparing both the gross profit margin and net profit margin we can arrive at a better conclusion.

## Return On Capital Employed (ROCE)

You can calculate the ROCE as follows:

### ROCE = Earnings before interest tax/ Capital employed

Capital employed = (debt + shareholders equity)/2

This approach measures the ability of the business to generate return on total capital employed.

Shareholders are the people who invest in the business with a certain amount of return for their investment. Additionally as a business owner you will also borrow to fund future expansion or refurbishment. So this ROCE calculates whether the business is generating sufficient return to cover the shareholders' expectations and interest expenses.

## Gearing ratio

You can calculate the gearing ratio as follows:

**Gearing = Total liabilities/Shareholders' equity**

This ratio measures the leverage position of the company. Generally 50% to 60% gearing level is an acceptable level. Anything beyond that level can lead to serious consequences, like the company struggling to make the interest payments and the bank taking over your assets.

## Current ratio

The current ratio is used to analyse the liquidity of the company. In simple terms it ascertain whether the business' short term assets are sufficient enough to cover its short term obligations. It can be calculated as follows:

**Current ratio = Current assets/Current liabilities**

A higher current ratio is not good for the company and vice versa. However, it is very important to understand that this is not only the liquidity measure of the company. Understanding the types of short term assets a company has and how quickly they can be converted into cash will give a better understanding about the company's liquidity position.

## How to Identify and Implement Your KPI

You must set strategic goals for your business. They can vary from business to business. For example: if you are running a business with a motive to make money, then your KPI will be based on profitability measures such as gross profit, pre-tax profit and so on.

On the other hand if you are running a not-for-profit organization your goal will be more focused on achieving non-profit measures such as the number of people who benefited from your organization, your contribution to social developments in the form building schools and so on.

It is very important to understand that KPI should be quantifiable. Once you set the target for your business you can easily implement set ideas to work towards that goal. Each year you can review your performance and can add more value to your shareholders.

### Balanced scorecard and its usefulness

Balanced scorecard is a strategic performance management framework that allows management to identify strategic priorities. According to these priorities, the management can design and implement goals and measures to evaluate how well they are executing their strategic goal. The balanced scorecard measures the organization performance in four metrics. They are:

- Financial perspective
- Customer perspective
- Internal perspective
- Learning and growth perspective

You can use a balanced scorecard to improve the organizational performance by aligning performance related pay with it. If the management achieves their target, they will be rewarded with a bonus; if not, they will not be rewarded a bonus and will be subject to investigation.

**For example** – you are running five burger shops in London, and they are managed by five different management teams. You identify that the performance in 2 shops was excellent the last two years, but currently has started to decline. For the rest of the burger shops the performances are steady but can be improved, as the burger shops are strategically located near schools, hospitals, and office complexes.

When you are investigating the reason for the deteriorating performance of the 2 shops with the management, they replied that the staff working in their shops are not motivated. The reason for this de-motivation is irrespective of their best performance during the last year, they have been treated similarly to the rest of the shops.

Now you have identified that there is a critical need

for performance related pay, and it is very important to implement it as soon as possible.

In order to implement this policy, you have identified 5 KPI of your business and planning to set a target for each KPI. The KPIs are sales, food cost, labour cost, customer service and net profit.

For each of these KPIs you have to set target measures which the management needs to achieve. Now let's find out how you can set the BSC.

The performance measures are set for a quarter:

Sales target £ 120,000

Food cost 30% of the sales

Labour cost 25% of the sales

Customer service target is to reduce the number of customer complaints to 10.

Net profit 10% of the sales

Now you should set points ranging from 0 to 1 for each target measure. If the management achieves the target they will be awarded 1 point; if not, 0 points will be awarded. Now the maximum points a store can achieve is 5 and the lowest is 0.

If a management team achieves 5 points they will be eligible for the high performance related pay. Achieving 4 points will enable them to get a bonus but it will be lower than the previous one. Anything below 4 points will not be eligible for a bonus. If the management scores below 1 or 2 they will be subject to investigation and proper actions should be taken to improve performance in future.

These target measures will motivate your team members to achieve the strategic goals. If you don't have a proper goal it can be really de-motivating for top performers in your company. You can always add more insights to these performance measures and can enhance shareholders' wealth.

## CHAPTER 7

# BASIC HR & PAYROLL

If you are preparing to hire your first employee, you should approach it with caution. It is very important to hire a suitable candidate to add value to your organization. The selected candidate should be trustworthy. Apart from those issues there are several legal factors which you should take into account when hiring new employees.

## Employing Staff for the First Time

In almost every country it is legally very important to meet the minimum wages, so before hiring anyone you should find out the minimum wages in your country. For example, in the UK, the minimum wage is £ 6.70 per hour for employees over 21 years old as of Oct 2015. If the legal body, which is the HMRC in the UK, finds out that you are not paying the minimum wages they will send you the arrears payment you have to make plus a penalty for not making minimum wages payments.

## Check the Legal Status to Work

This is critical when you are hiring foreign workers. Some of them might be students and their work hours will be limited to certain hours. You can research their work rights on the VISA page. If you are unable to find out, please feel free to contact legal bodies to find out their working rights.

## Obtain Employer's Liability Insurance

You should get your employer's liability insurance coverage as soon as you have registered yourself as an employer. This liability coverage is useful when your employees have injured themselves at work or if they get work-related illness such as stress and so on.

## Terms and Conditions of the Employment

You should give written statements of employment contract to your employee. This should clearly communicate the roles and responsibilities of the selected candidate.

Sometimes as an employer you may need to invest a huge amount in training. If the selected candidate leaves after the training process, your loss is severe. In these instances you can specify the penalty payments the employee needs to make before leaving and the period of notice they have to give.

## Registering your Business as an Employer

You have to register your business as an employer with the legal entity in your country. For example, in the UK you have to register yourself with the HMRC as an employer. After registering yourself, the HMRC will send you the PAYE reference number and accounts office reference.

**Easy way to learn payroll is to install any free trial version of the payroll software and learn the following.**

Pay system
Codes
Procedures
Sick Pay
Maternity
Benefits
Schemes
Set Up Employees
Process salaries
Leavers and Starters
Statutory Sick Pay and Maternity Pay
Loans and Holiday Pay
Year End Records

## CHAPTER 8

# SAY YES TO ACCOUNTING SYSTEM

There are free trial version available for most of the accounting software such as Sage Line 50, Quick book. You can refer to the user guide and

- Learn how sage integrates the ledgers and records double entries

- Learn about VAT accounting setup methods

- Learn how to enter customer's opening balances

- Learn how to enter a new customer

- Learn how to enter suppliers' opening balances

- Learn how to enter a new supplier

- Learn how to backup accounts data

- Learn how to restore accounts data onto Sage

- Learn how to enter opening balances onto the nominal ledger

- Learn how to prepare and print a trial balance

- Learn how to change the program date

- Learn how to make stock adjustments

- Learn how to enter supplier invoices

- Learn how to batch of supplier invoices

- Learn how to post error corrections

- Learn how to amend/add to existing customer and supplier records

- Learn how to create customer invoices

- Learn how to preview/print customer invoices

- Learn how to check activity on customer accounts

- Learn how to update ledgers

- Learn how to create customer letters

- Learn how to enter new product details

- Learn how to enter customer receipts for invoiced items

- Learn how to enter bank receipts for non-invoiced items

- Learn how to enter a customer receipt as part payment

- Learn how to check the activity of an account following part payment

- Learn how to access customer and supplier process windows

- Learn how to produce statements for customers

- Learn how to process payments made against supplier invoices

- Learn how to process bank payments for non-invoiced items

- Learn how to enter petty cash

payments

- Learn how to use bank transfer to restore the petty cash float

- Learn how to use a journal to correct errors

- Learn how to a use journal to update the accounts with payroll details

- Learn how to add a new nominal account

- Learn the role of the Chart of Accounts, and how to amend it

- Learn how to reconcile the bank statement

- Learn how to print & view bank reports and day books

- Learn how to use criteria to view specific reports

- Learn how to print out the audit trail

- Learn how to correct basic entry errors

- Learn how to reconcile the debtors and

creditors control accounts

- Learn how to delete obsolete customer and supplier records

- Learn how to set up a customer to receive settlement discount

- Learn how to use memorise and recall in the batch supplier invoice window

- Learn how to enter budget information and create departments

- Learn how to create sales credit notes

- Learn how to process purchase credit notes

- Learn how to adjust stock records for returns

- Learn how to post a payment on account

- Learn how to allocate a payment on account

- Learn how to process a receipt that includes settlement discount

- Learn how to use memorise and recall in the bank window

- Learn how to process petty cash

- Learn how to set up a recurring entry

- Learn how to delete a recurring entry

- Learn how to enter journals

- Learn how to check and reconcile the VAT return

- Learn how to use the VAT transfer wizard

- Learn how to produce profit & loss and balance sheet

## CHAPTER 9

# BENEFITS OF VIRTUAL BOOKKEEPING IN THE DIGITAL AGE

### What is Virtual Bookkeeping?

Virtual bookkeeping is where a professionally qualified accountant carries out your routine bookkeeping virtually. It can be carried out from a home or any part of the world.

### How They Work

The basic requirement for this operation is a high-speed internet connection and access to cloud accounting software.

Once you set up a cloud network for your company, the bookkeeper will access your server to perform the necessary tasks. Alternatively, you can totally outsource your bookkeeping to be managed from their server and perform all the work for you.

**Send your financial data**

- Bank statements
- Supplier invoices
- Payroll iformation
- Other informations

**Accounting Tasks will be performed**

- Enter all transactions
- Process payroll
- Bank reconciliation
- VAT return
- Other necessary tasks

**Real time Accounting Solutions**

- Monthly management accounts
- Cashflow forecasting
- Age creditors report
- And more

## Benefits of switching to virtual accountants

**Cost reduction** – we are all affected by the economic crisis. Every business is under severe pressure to cut costs. A virtual accountant is the gateway to reduce your business costs.

Instead of running a team of 5 accountants, you can choose to hire one accountant and the rest is done with a virtual accountant. The cost saving will be almost by 50% however this is subject to your business models and complexities. Using these savings in cost, you can invest in business developments. This will helps you to grow your business rapidly.

Secondly, a virtual accountant reduces the hardware and upgrade costs.

Thirdly, you can use the office space to implement a sales team or other professional team members who really take part in the end products or services delivered to the customers.

**Focus on core competence** – if you are an entrepreneur you should focus on your core competence and how you can add more value

to the end products or services. If you focus more on accounting during the initial stages, you may be overtaken by your competitors. So your virtual accountant helps you to focus on key business principles and enhancing the value addition to the customers. You don't need to worry about staff leaving or holiday coverage, etc.

**Flexibility** – virtual accounting is very flexible. You can hire virtual accountants based on your requirements: on a weekly basis, monthly basis, or yearly basis.

**Anytime anywhere access** – as we all are in the information age, the real benefit of virtual accounting is you can access it from your business, home, or any part of the world. This access enables you to make better decisions on time.

**Qualified Accountants** – you could have a team made up of people of top caliber in the accounting profession, holding professional qualifications such as CIMA, ACCA, ACA, CPA, etc., and exposure to the big four firms is also great value addition to your business model.

### Is your confidentially being compromised?

The main question behind a third party virtual accountant is whether confidentiality is being compromised.

It is fair to say that a business' key information can fall in to the wrong party's hands, such as competitors or the media. The consequences may be severe depending on the information which is leaked. You have to make sure each and every staff member is obliged to follow the ethical codes, which is to meet client confidentiality.

A **Service Level Agreement (SLA)** can be developed to protect your confidentiality when you have decided to move along with a third party accountant. The service level agreement can classify the duties and responsibilities of each party. It can also be done with the help of lawyers.

### What happens when the server crashes?

By conducting regular backups you will be protected from server crashes. The backups can be done on a weekly basis, and you can create a separate folder to keep your backup files. When the system crashes you can use your backup files.

### How to Choose Your Service Level Package

You have to shop around and choose a customised package to meet your requirements. Running a business is not only about bookkeeping; you should be able to identify the key performance indicators in your business, internal control weakness, how to reduce the borrowing cost, and so on.

As an entrepreneur or start-up you will be facing cash flow issues in hiring a Chief Financial Officer (CFO). In order to fill this gap you can negotiate and ask for your Cloud CFO, who will be assisting you and will be providing you with the necessary financial advisory services.

## Benefits of Having Your Cloud CFO with Virtual Bookkeeping Services

• Hiring a CFO to assist you is expensive. Having access to Free CFO advice when required will be enough during the start-up period until you grow bigger.

• You will have a good reporting structure which highlights your business performance.

• It is not about just bookkeeping. Monthly performance reviews can be very useful to boost your business.

• Monthly management accounting – this can clearly highlight your profit margin, labour and food cost as a percentage of sales, and so on.

• Control weaknesses and risk assessment – it is very important to place tight internal controls and external systems in place. Without these systems, even if you make sufficient money you cannot run your business in the long run. The CFO will recommend to you the possible systems you can implement to control your weaknesses.

- Cash flow forecasting – the main purpose of running a business is to enhance shareholders' wealth. In order to do so you should always plan your income and expenses in advance. This will help you to control unnecessary borrowings, cheques bouncing, or poor relationships with suppliers due to not releasing payments on time.

- Investment appraisal – as you grow you may need to buy new business ventures. You can ask your Cloud CFO to assist you in valuing the business using several techniques, such as free cash flow, EV multiples and so on. This valuation will stop you from paying too much for a buyout.

- The CFO will also highlight for you the potential synergies available to you via mergers and acquisitions.

- Unbiased decision making – decision making is one of the keys to the success of a business, and should be made on time. An in-house CFO might make decisions to maximise his own wealth. But with the use of your Cloud CFO, this biased decision making is eliminated. Your Cloud CFO will recommend to you the most suitable cause of action plans for your business needs.

## CHAPTER 10

# WHAT'S STOPPING YOU?

### (1) Failure to recognise exactly what you want

What you enjoy most? You have to identify your passion first. You have to enjoy what you're doing to be able to achieve long term success. This would give you personal satisfaction, financial gain, enjoyment and stability. You have to truly believe in yourself and you have to do it with full commitment.

### (2) Procrastination

Are you finding excuses for doing it in the future or waiting for the right time to start? Start NOW!! Procrastination permits your mind and body to switch off from being productive. Procrastination will reduce your self-esteem and will also lower your reputation in the eyes of others. This needs to be solved with immediate effect by making sure you take necessary action.

## (3) Fear of failure and criticism

What others will think about you? Ignore it. A state of mind is something that one assumes. It is not something that can be purchased, but something that has to be created. The "FEARS" are sufficient enough to destroy your chances of achieving a high standard in any undertaking. They will wipe out your passion and make self-control impossible, lead to indecision, discourage creativity and encourage procrastination. You have to come out from your comfort zone and overcome all types of fears.

## (4) Lack of interest in learning and acquiring some knowledge for your own future.

Education is an on-going process. You have to attend seminars, workshops, and training courses. You have to read books, magazines, reports, journals, newsletters, websites and industry publications in your own field. You have to always think of innovative ways to do things better in less time with less effort. You have to educate yourself with essential skills.

You have to become known as an expert in your field. Don't waste time, energy and money. Always focus on improving yourself, stimulating ideas, sharing ideas, listening to others, talking about the project, and working with collaborators.

## (5) Habit of relying on others instead of creating a plan to find the solution to the problem yourself

If you want to achieve success you have to work hard. It's your life. No point of blaming others or relying on others. You have to stop the habit of blaming others for mistakes rather than taking responsibility. If you believe yourself and rely on yourself, success will follow.

## (6) Lack of organised plan. Habit of compromising poverty instead of aiming riches

If you fail to plan you plan to fail. You have to set your goals. You have to set your long-term, medium-term and short-term goals, then create an action plan to reach those goals by creating step-by-step, measurable stages.

## (7) Habit of neglecting to move on ideas or to grasp an opportunity.

You have to develop a winning attitude and have to be very open-minded person, which will help you to spot opportunities and also to turn your failures into successes.

*"If there is a God, he is within. You don't ask God to give you things; you depend on God for your inner theme."*

– Bruce Lee

## (8) Not believing in yourself

Believes make your reality. Never give up on your dreams and beliefs as you will never know how worthy you are until you actually put them into action.

*"Working hard is important, but there is something that matters even more: Believe in yourself."* – Harry Potter

## (9) Not willing to change

You have to be the change rather than trying to change the world. Change has to start within ourselves; we cannot expect the world to change if we do not. Instead of focusing on problems, we can start to live solutions. You have the ability, capacity, capability, resources, strength, and wisdom to not only makes changes but to become the change you longed for.

## (10) Lack of persistence

Persistence is the ability to stick with something. The majority of people face failure due to lack of persistence in creating alternative plans to take the place of those which fail.

*"Patience, persistence and perspiration make an unbeatable combination for success"*

-Napoleon Hill

## CHAPTER 11

# WHO YOU KNOW?

## TOP 10 BENEFITS OF NETWORKING:

### 1) Opens the Door to Connect and Talk to Highly Influential People.

Reaching highly influenced individuals is very difficult in normal conditions.

*"It's not WHAT you know, but WHO you know"*

### 2) Increases the Chance of Getting Suitable Jobs

In current economic climate, job market is very competitive. Therefore highly influential connections would increase the chances of referrals for jobs.

### 3) Your Confidence Level Will Increase

Regular networking would help you to push yourself to talk to people you don't know and you will get increased confidence the more you do this.

## 4) Positive Influence and Positive Energy

It is important to be surrounding yourself with positive, uplifting people that help you to grow. The people that you hang around with and talk to do influence who you are and what you do.

## 5) New Opportunities will Come to You

Opportunities within networking are really endless such as joint ventures, clients, business partnerships, speaking, writing opportunities and so on. You should not jump into all opportunities. Have a vision and set goals. Then use networking to find the right opportunities.

## 6) Improved Decision Making

If you want to be really successful, then you need to have a great source of relevant connections in your network that you can call when needed to make the right decision.

## 7) Raising Your Profile and Reputation

Build your reputation as a knowledgeable, reliable and supportive person by offering useful information or tips to people. Being visible and getting noticed is a big benefit of networking.

## 8) Knowledge Sharing

Networking is great for sharing ideas and knowledge and allows you to see things from another perspective. Whether it's asking for feedback or discussing your point of view, it will help you expand your knowledge and would help to avoid making the same mistakes again. This will save lots of time and money.

## 9) Develop Your Skills

Networking would increase your communication, presentation, time management, team working, leadership and problem solving skills by talking with lots of new people in different areas.

## 10) Personal Satisfaction of Helping Others

Everyone has their own problems. And all problems can be solved. Networking would give an opportunity to help other people to solve their problems. You should not expect anything in return for the advice. For each and every help you do you will automatically get the return in some form. Personal satisfaction of helping others is the biggest return.

## CHAPTER 12

# HOW TO USE LINKEDIN TO BUILD YOUR PROFESSIONAL BRAND

**1) Your photo**

LinkedIn profile picture should be a professional photo

**2) Your headline**

Try to stand out by stating what you have to offer and identifying your unique selling point to attract recruiters.

Examples:

DO: Accounting Graduate, Specialising in management Accounting.

Interested in strategic decision making

DON'T: Motivated Graduate Looking to Work in Accounting

## 3) Your summary

You should focus on what you want to do and include achievements to attract a lot of eyeballs. You could upload a short video clip where you talk about yourself.

## 4) Your keywords

The more industry-relevant keywords you have in your profile, the higher you are on a recruiter's search rankings. This increases the chances of your profile getting noticed.

## 5) Your education section

This is an important networking tool, which would help you to connect with your alumni.

## 6) Claim your vanity URL

Personalise the web address for your LinkedIn profile this would help you appear on Google, if employers search for you

## 7) Your public profile settings:

Go to your public profile and set visible on your public profile. I would recommend having the summary, your current position, skills and education visible.

## 8) Your connections

Connecting with all students would help to find out how other college graduates found a job or got hired by an employer.

You can import your email list to find out who among your friends is present on LinkedIn.

You also can connect with people outside of your network. You can do an introduction through a common connection

## 9) Join Groups

By joining the larger groups, with the most number of members, you can increase your potential network. Take part in group discussions. You can even start discussions asking for advice related to your job search, such as recommendations for good courses, training and vacancies.

## 10) Get Recommendations

If you have more recommendations, you will have a great chance of attracting the employers' attention.

## 11) Set Job Alerts

Helpful for you to receive notifications of recommended jobs. Employers post vacancies with the hope of jobseeker like you will come across them and turn out to be the ideal candidate.

## 12) Post status update daily

This will increase your visibility. If you do have a Twitter account, you can integrate into your LinkedIn account to get more audience.

## 13) Use applications to reach more audience

SlideShare to share presentations of your company or about specials or promotions you have on at the moment,

Google Docs to get video going on your profile

Blog Link application for bloggers

This would attract employer's attention and increase the chances of a company inviting you for an interview or referral from other professionals.

## 14) Find suitable events to attend

You can find the relevant events on Linkedin by using key words search. This would help you meet professionals in person would open new opportunities.

LinkedIn would help you to get largest connection of global professional network, improved personal brand, improved recognition, improved visibility, new opportunities, etc

## CHAPTER 13

# CV WRITING TIPS

1) Identify what qualifies you for the role

2) Select a simple and standardized format, don't go for anything too fancy.

3) Please double check and make sure your contact information is accurate and up-to-date with a primary contact number, a mobile phone number and email address. Put your name and contact details at the top of the page, then use the job title itself as a heading. Under this, summarise key details such experience in a particular skill, project experience or a short branding statement highlighting your strengths and attributes. Include a brief cover letter explaining your reasons for applying, and interest in the company.

4) Include an objective statement to tell the

employer about your strongest and most desirable personality is applicable to the job you are applying for.

5) If you have no work experience, not to worry. List your volunteer work or community activities or work experience through a course at school or course work at school that you feel is relevant to the job, career oriented education and any academic achievements or awards. Explain how you think your excellent performance in these areas would benefit the employer and enhance your ability to do the job. Try to get a letter of reference from a teacher of one of the courses you mention.

6) Think from the employer's perspective. Decide on the most interesting factors, where you have used relevant skills, and then make these prominent on your CV. Voluntary or community involvement, work placements, coursework, personal projects and extracurricular activities can all be highlighted to show your suitability.

7) Think of any project that you undertook at School or University or Personal, which is relevant to this job. Break down your projects into target, result and learned competencies to shows relevant skills, achievements, ability to get on with others, organisational and communication skills.

8) Quantify your achievements where possible such as how much money saved, percentage of time reduced, etc

9) Try to use keywords such as decision making, risk management, etc under skills and work experience section.

10) If you have a position of authority in any of the groups make note of it and describe your duties.

11) **List any awards you've received or the subjects you've excelled at in school.** Awards are not easy to get, thus they show commitment and hard work.

12) Use action-oriented words to describe responsibilities.

- Innovated
- Motivated
- Facilitated
- Organized
- Managed

13) Please make the most of your qualities such as your skills, attitude, potential and enthusiasm.

14) Don't lie and always be true to who you are.

15) Make yourself look good. It's not lying.

For example, if you were the person at your previous job to clean up the mess at the end of the day, you might say that as follows:

"I have facilitated teamwork by organizing the work site more efficiently". This is not lying.

16) Sell yourself by making a list of your skills, special talents, or positive personality traits.

17) When writing your first resume don't make it more than a page. Employers will not expect a long work history from a first time worker.

18) Put the most important information first. You don't need to always use a strict chronological work history format. Relevant project work can come before less relevant employment.

19) Find great references.

Your teacher or previous employer or adviser can also be great references. Only pick contacts who will say good things about you.

20) Talk to your contacts in advance and coach them slightly on the nature of the job and what you are applying for.

## CHAPTER 14

# INTERVIEW SUCCESS

### 1. Dress for Success

You have to invest in a good professional outfit. Make sure your shoes are polished and professional-looking. Choose a suitable colour to boost your professional image. Do not go for bright colours as it may distract the interviewer from the actual perspective of the interview. If you dress well this will automatically increase your self-confidence on the day.

### 2. Transferable Skills

Most companies would want their employees to be versatile, be able to know the ins and outs of any role. Be able to work as a team player and have the passion to want to succeed in everything that they undertake.

### 3. Grades Don't Matter

The key when it comes to interviews is that degrees

don't matter. The interviewer would be more focused on your experience and expertise. Your personality will play a key role in the selection process.

A good tip: before you put your foot into the industry, you should always try and get maximal amount of experience in a variety of fields, be it paid or voluntary. The key is to always keep on learning and expanding on your knowledge to be able to pass down to younger generations for history to commence.

## 4. Fresh New Ideas

You have to be innovative. The interviewers will look for employees who will bring them in the maximal amount of profit in the future. So think outside the box.

## 5. Prepare and Practice

Spend time researching the company by visiting their website. Make sure you read up on their annual report, mission statement, products, services, management team, hierarchy, Linkedin profile, etc. Purpose of the interview is not to tell them about yourself but it's the opportunity to show that you can add value to the organization. Therefore make sure you're prepared.

## 6. Stay Cool and Calm

Interviewers will know that most people will be nervous during their interview so always try and stay calm. Make sure that you answer all your questions with confidence. This will differentiate you among the other candidates and make sure you stand out from the crowd.

Your body language is a vital part of the interview. Make sure that you are not fidgeting with your fingers or shaking your leg. To prevent this from happening it may be wise to have you fingers locked, with your back straight so you're not slouching on the chair. Sit in a professional manner and focus and listen carefully as to what the interviewers are asking you. Keep eye contact at all times.

## 7. Be Yourself

Never try to be someone that you're not at the interview. By giving false impressions you are leading them to think that you're someone that you're not. This will cause problems in the long run resulting in disappointment. The interviewers are always impressed by the ones who are honest and true to themselves as well as having the willingness to learn attitude. Remember skills can be trained but not attitude.

## 8. Ask Questions

When the interviewer invites you to ask questions always do so. Remember that an interview is not a test it's a two way conversation, where on one side the interviewer is trying to determine whether you're the correct candidate for their job role whereas on the other hand you're trying to determine whether this is the correct job role for you. For example: Would there be any progression within the job role? etc

## 9. Send a Thank You Email and Follow Up on the Outcome

Always ensure that you follow up after your interview by sending a thank you email. This will give a lasting impression and place you ahead of the crowd.

## CHAPTER 15

# HOW TO ANSWER INTERVIEW QUESTIONS

### 1. Can you tell me a little about yourself?

Don't give your complete employment or personal history. Instead just give a pitch saying exactly why you're the right fit for the job. Start off with the 2-3 specific accomplishments or experiences that you most want the interviewer to know about, and then wrap up talking about how that prior experience has placed you for this specific role.

### 2. How did you hear about the position?

This is actually a perfect opportunity to stand out and show your passion for and connection to the company. For example, if you found out about this job through a friend or professional contact, name drop that person, then share why you were so excited about it, specifically, caught your eye about the role.

## 3. What do you know about the company?

Try to show them you care about it the company mission and goals.

## 4. Why do you want this job?

Companies want to hire people who are passionate about the job, so you should have a great answer about why you want the position. Identify the key factors that make the role a great fit for you. For example "I think you guys are doing great on customer service and business expansion, so I want to be a part of it"

## 5. Why should we hire you?

Sell yourself and your skills to the hiring manager. You can not only do the work, you can deliver great results. You'll really fit in with the team and culture and that you'd be a better hire than any of the other candidates.

## 6. What are your greatest professional strengths?

Share your true strengths that are most targeted to this particular position.

## 7. What do you consider to be your weaknesses?

Objective is to identify your self-awareness and honesty. Say something that you struggle with but that you're working to improve. For example, maybe you've never been strong at public speaking, but you've recently volunteered to run meetings to help you be more comfortable when addressing a crowd.

## 8. What is your greatest professional achievement?

Nothing says "hire me" better than a track record of achieving amazing results in past jobs, so don't be shy when answering this question! A great way to do so is by using the S-T-A-R method:

Set up the situation

Task that you were required to complete

Action you have taken

Result archived.

## 9. Tell me about a challenge or conflict you've faced at work, and how you dealt with it.

Objective is to find out how you will respond to conflict.

Use S-T-A-R method, being sure to focus on how you handled the situation professionally and productively, and ideally closing with a happy ending, like how you came to a resolution or compromise.

## 10. Where do you see yourself in five years?

Objective of this question is to find out whether you have set realistic expectations for your career and also to find out whether you have ambition which aligns with your goals and growth

## 11. What's your dream job?

Interviewer wants to uncover whether this position is really in line with your ultimate career goals. Talk about your goals and ambitions and why this job will get you closer to them.

## 12. What other companies are you interviewing with?

Objective is to find out what the competition is for

you? And also to find out whether you're serious about the industry

## 13. Why are you leaving your current job?

Keep things positive. You have nothing to gain by being negative about your past employers. Shows that you're eager to take on new opportunities and that the role you're interviewing for is a better fit for you than your current or last position. For example, "I'd really love to be part of blue chip senior management team and I know I'd have that opportunity here." If you can position the learning experience as an advantage for this next job, even better.

## 14. What are you looking for in a new position? What type of work environment do you prefer?

Be specific. List same things that this position has to offer Mention similar to the environment of the company you're applying to.

## 15. What were your bosses' strengths/weaknesses?

They want to see how you handle tough questions.

They want to hear something positive

They want to know your weakness won't affect your performance.

## 16. What's your management style?

The best managers are strong but flexible; I tend to approach my employee relationships as a coach. Share a couple of your best managerial moments, like when you grew your team from 2 to 10 or coached an underperforming employee to become the company's top salesperson.

## 17. What's a time you exercised leadership?

Choose an example that showcases your project management skills and ability to confidently and effectively lead a team.

## 18. What's a time you disagreed with a decision that was made at work?

Objective is to find out whether you can do so in a productive, professional way. Tell the one where your actions made a positive difference on the outcome of the situation, whether it was a work-related outcome or a more effective and productive working relationship.

## 19. How would your boss and co-workers describe you?

Tell about your strength, your strong work ethic or your willingness to work in on any projects when needed.

## 20. If you have a gap in your employment

I decided to take a break at the time for impressive volunteer/ blogging or taking classes but today I'm ready to contribute to this organization in the following ways."

## 21. If you have changed career paths

Give a few examples of how your past experience is transferrable to the new role.

## 22. How do you deal with pressure or stressful situations?

Choose an answer that shows that you can meet a stressful situation head-on in a productive, positive manner and let nothing stop you from accomplishing your goal. By making to-do list

## 23. What would your first 30, 60, or 90 days look like in this role?

What you'd need to do to get ramped up.

What information would you need?

What parts of the company would you need to familiarize yourself with?

What other employees would you want to sit down with?

Choose a couple of areas where you think you can make meaningful contributions right away.

## 24. What are your salary requirements?

State the highest number in that range that applies based on your experience, education, and skills. Then tell you want the job and are willing to negotiate.

## 25. What do you like to do outside of work?

Objective is to see whether you will fit in with the culture and gives you the opportunity to open up and display their personality too.

## 26. Who are our competitors? What do you think we could do better or differently?

Please carry out enough research about the company. Whether you have some background on the company and you're able to think critically about it and come to the table with new ideas. How could the company increase profit/ improve customer service.

## 27. What motivates you?

If you're someone that loves a challenge, then maybe mentioning that you're at your most motivated when faced with unforeseen or even expected challenges and overcoming them would be a good idea.

If you're interviewing for a Social Media Manager role, you could say that helping customers and engaging with fans motivates you to do your best every day), but there are certain answers you can give which apply to any job, however these should be customised to the position you're interviewing for.

For example, if you thrive on coming up with new ways of approaching tasks or projects, then saying that being innovative and finding new, more effective ways of working motivates you would be a good answer.

## 28. What's your availability?

- Don't leave your current job without sufficient notice to your employer.

- Don't give notice to your current employer until you are holding a written job offer – that you have accepted, preferably in writing – in your hands.

## 29. Would you work 40+ hours a week?

Objective is to find out whether you got time management skills to finish the task on time and also whther you can work more hours if needed. i.e some urgent tasks with tight deadline

## 30. Do you have any questions for us?

It's your opportunity to sniff out whether a job is the right fit for you. What do you want to know about the position? The company? The department? The team? What can you tell me about your new products or plans for growth?

.

## CHAPTER 16

# OPPORTUNITIES AND YOU

Currently the world faces economic crisis and unemployment issues. Especially after 9/11 we have started to hear the term coined by economists and thought to be the most dreaded expression in English (at least in the frame of reference of the Economist): "economic crisis." It cannot be refuted that a lot of developed countries have faced a depression in their economic outlook, and this has also paved the way for unemployment issues in these countries. This is in fact viewed by the public as a crisis or problem; however is this same public that has used the phrase "in testing time lies opportunity." This phrase has been used by motivational speakers and coaches for a long time. However, it is not just a motivational phrase; it is in fact plain truth. The economy is dynamic, innovative, and creates the necessary jobs which require a greater number of young people who are willing and able to become entrepreneurs, who will launch and successfully develop their own commercial or social ventures, or who will become innovators in the wider organisations in which they work. You should not blindly follow what is already in practice; everything depends on how creative, innovative, well-educated, and well-informed the market is. There have been several companies who have nailed this and have become successful in testing times. Examples of organisations who have taken advantage of difficult times, relished them, and fought back to succeed by identifying the gaps and opportunities are Foursquare (started in 2009), and Twitter (started in 2006). So what made them succeed? Their education certainly influenced their attitude, skills and moulded the culture for them to act on their feet. This independent thinking, as well the creative desire, paved way to entrepreneurial thinking from a young age. In addition, consider the number of entrepreneurs who act as role models for the youth of today in the form of thought leaders and mentors.

As important as it is to be creative, innovative and look forward towards the future, it is also imperative that we look at the past and assess what has created success, what has worked for people, when and why they made such a move, and how they did it. We should carefully analyse the technological breakthroughs and learn from them, and it goes without saying that it is this practice that sparked a lot of entrepreneurial ideas within the successful businesses we have heard of.

The industrial revolution in the 1700s was due to the industrial units which were powered by heavy machineries, and the invention of trains and ships. And then in the 1870s, Alexander Graham Bell invented the telephone, which enabled us to communicate through voice no matter where we were; this was the seed for a business to operate in multiple locations and still remain connected to their head office. By the 1900s, the travel industry was further boosted by the invention of objects of flight which we fondly call aeroplanes; however, it is another story that these planes were also used for warfare purposes. The factory line (or assembly line) system, which was conceptualised in 1913, made the factory worker's process similar to that of a well-oiled machine. This led the organisations to cater to mass market and achieve economies of scale. The invention of machines did not stop there: by the 1930s, even farming activities were revolutionized with the invention of the combine harvester, giving the farmer more time to focus on other activities. And the invention that first enabled people to learn information within a matter of few hours, the television, was invented. The automobile industry, the pharmaceutical industry, the personal computer, from the old commodore machines to the new sleek tablet PCs, the internet (world wide web), mobile phones, and finally all the technological gadgets that influence and transform our day-to-day life, which in turn resulted in the evolution of our culture, attitudes and beliefs. Google changed the internet and the way of doing business in 1998 by making the whole web searchable. Now by using the search engine, you were able to find anything you want, search about anyone you are interested in, find answers for any question you have, and what's more, you were able to do all this in a matter of seconds.

This paved way for many more companies swarming into what we now call the SaaS industry, or in other words virtual business. This has fulfilled the dream of staff and customers being anywhere in the world still being able to do business. Work can be done from home, teams can be spread out worldwide, and no one cares. This ability has resulted in an immense difference between the haves and have-nots in the world, and in the drastic mismatch in the economic prowess of countries. People who have thought ahead of the time and also learnt from the past have motored ahead, while others are still lagging behind. These innovations expanded human intellect, increased the life expectancy in the United States through newly developed medicines, and at the same time kept more than 1 billion people from starving.

Have you stopped to think why this happened? Through forward thinking, people who could afford to buy machines multiplied their wealth and made enormous fortunes. Those who didn't have the means went to the factory floor to become faceless and nameless corporate slaves.

We can blame the industrial revolution, which taught the workers and controlled them by planting the idea that by suffering now, they will be able to reap benefits in the future. Often times, people did accept this idea, dropped their independent ideas, and went on working like machines. Our educational institutes too were tasked with creating obedient workers, not entrepreneurs. Before the industrial revolution, people did not create large businesses, but they had a wild imagination and the dream to experiment, they knew what they wanted to do, and both the customers and the entrepreneurs knew each other by name. There was a spirit of entrepreneurship within each individual.

In the early days of the industrial revolution, not everyone was able to set up a factory, owing to the costs that were involved in establishing such a business. However, in today's terms, a person with a mobile phone, a Facebook page, a laptop, and a decent idea can be a winner. These are businesses which have one owner, one worker, and one beneficiary – and the new breed of entrepreneur have arrived. The UK is known for its high number of home bakers, and each one of them is an example of how they fit into this new breed. Another advantage for these small budding companies is that it makes it easy for them to reinvent themselves, refine themselves, and be agile in decision making, because they are small and it does not take a long time to implement the changes compared to large companies. Almost a decade ago, Nokia, was the most innovative company; however, things changed after they expanded. Now they are struggling to catch up with Apple and Samsung. People will matter again, causes will matter again, and maybe we will see a world that works for a lot more people.

In the Entrepreneur Revolution, your most valued

asset is your personal brand and reputation. When somebody googles your name, the first page of results is a perfect indication of how the world sees you.

I would like to stress again, the world has changed, and it will continue to change and evolve. The internet has played a large part in this, and has given new powers to every individual who uses it correctly. An example would be the success of "Gangnam Style" by Psy. Psy was unheard of, and what more, K-Pop was restricted to Korea. But within Psy and his team there was mastery in using social media, and this created the unprecedented success for the song which generated millions of dollars. In similar terms, the internet and its facilities has enabled people to host their own podcasts, video blogs, TV channels, and radio channels, and all these are being used to sell merchandise. All that is necessary is a good idea and a creative way of getting it across, and when I say getting it across, it means globally. People in Asia watch the video channel of 'Super Woman' on YouTube; the views range in the millions, and people spend money buying her merchandise. The evolution of technology allows you to make money from tiny, silly little ideas. Radically, it allows people to make money from their passions.

Of course technology itself is not the answer to the success of ventures; it is part of the reason for the success. While being focused on technology, entrepreneurs also paid enough attention to sales, marketing, product development, management, and business development. This was the result of determination, passion, and drawing inspiration from little successes. This is the simplest of recipes to create and instil an entrepreneur within you. Entrepreneurs know that you have to find a problem, and the solution to that problem will be the product you need to develop. Mere identification won't work, you need to manage the development and see to it that it is accomplished.

When you set up your own business, you have to take some time to carefully think and decide on the following:

- What type of free gift would you give without expecting any return?
- How to try out your service without committing to too much money or time.
- The way to obtain accurate contact information from your potential customers so that they could be offered with your services in the near future, enabling them to be retained as your permanent customers.

Then your core product can deliver a full solution to what people want and seriously solve problems.

You should always under-promise and over-deliver. If you focus on creating success for your clients, they will go out and tell the world.

The industrial age is over. We are living in the digital age, which is also known as the information age. Lots of people are still thinking and living in the industrial age. In the industrial age, people worry about lifetime job security. Even the educational systems of schools and universities were created to fulfil the needs of the industrial age, which were 9 to 5 workers who live their entire lives with the job security to look after their families without looking for more opportunities and without finding their actual ability, capacity and capabilities. This situation is similar to "a frog in the well," where we're not aware of the world outside the well. We all live in our comfort zone. Our parents, school, friends and society influence us a lot and thus we are unable to come out of our comfort zone. In order to do so, we have to exploit new opportunities to inspire the future.

This industrial to information age shift triggered the urgent need of raising more entrepreneurial leaders to solve economic crises. You all need to come out from your comfort zone to see the opportunities. There are plenty of opportunities in the world. This is the wake up call to become an entrepreneur to spot opportunities and act to make them into commercial successes.

**In the Dark Age,** you were not born to live your life as a slave. But most did.

**In the Agricultural Age,** you were not born to live

your life as a farmer. But most people did.

**In the Industrial Age,** you were not born to live your life as a factory worker. But most people did.

**Now we are in the Information Age.** You should not make the same mistakes again and again. You were born to **LIVE YOUR LIFE** where anything is possible for you. You can spot the right opportunities and make them successful to live your life happily and inspire others and the future generation.

**You always have to** do something you're passionate about. Do something you're good at and do something that makes money. A passionate person attracts opportunities like a magnet.

## CHAPTER 17

# INCREASE YOUR MIND POWER THROUGH SPIRITUAL ENERGY

Earth's population has surpassed 7 billion as I write this chapter, with an overall life expectancy of 69.92 years. There are more than 190 countries on earth, including the newly formed South Sudan. Each country and its people have different culture and different beliefs, they look different, they talk differently, they work differently; in short, they come from very diverse backgrounds. But, as many gurus have noted in the past, there is a common aspect in each and every one of us, and this is true irrespective of our religion, our language, our faith, our gender, our financial and social status, our aspirations, and our beliefs. That common aspect is that as human beings, all of us want to be HAPPY. But, if we consider if we have all been successful in achieving this, I must say NO, we have made a mistake in this regard. More often than not, we have been wasting a lot of time looking for this happiness in the external environment, whereas it would have been the best choice to spend that time to tap into the bliss within. Heraclitus quoted, *"The Only Thing That Is Constant Is Change,"* which will stand forever. The environment around us will keep on changing, and it is our mistake if we keep expecting to find happiness from the world around us. We should adopt and prepare ourselves to find permanent happiness, and for this we must realise that it is in the soul within that we must invest in to experience eternal happiness.

It is a rough stone that, when identified and uncovered by humans, goes through the process of cutting and polishing before we have in our hands the most precious of stones in the world: the diamond. Before it undergoes that process, it resembles just another stone. Similarly each individual has a bright light of enlightening within us, but it is covered with blankets of worldly needs and is hidden from us. It is this state that makes it difficult for us to find the true state of bliss, and paves the way to spiritual ignorance. Due to this, our mind does not look beyond the five senses. So how have a few people been able to find the bliss within them? This is where meditation, yoga, and recreational activities can help. These are activities that stimulate the search within yourself, where you spend quality time alone, exploring your thoughts, and defining yourself. The practicing of spirituality leads to permanent personality changes, whereby the individual becomes positive in their approach; there will always be a calm approach to every situation (no matter how demanding the situation is), the aura and charisma become infectious, and soon people will want the individual to be their role model and mentor.

Gautama Buddha was a spiritual leader; his teachings laid the foundation for modern day Buddhism. Buddha lived a good portion of his early life in luxury, and once he ventured outside the palace walls, he saw the troubles which will eventually consume all human beings: suffering. To find solutions to the human condition, he initially lived a purely ascetic lifestyle, one in which he did not seek any material comfort or luxury. This lifestyle did not give him mental comfort; this extreme asceticism didn't work. Therefore, Buddha came to the conclusion that one has to live life the "middle way." This meant not too much materialistic comfort and not too much severe asceticism.

*"All that we are is the result of what we have thought. The mind is everything. What we think, we become."*
**– Buddha**

So what does Buddhism teach us? What does Buddha's life teach the leaders of today? What should be the summary to take away? Buddhism was conceptualised by Buddha with the aim of teaching a balanced life for humankind. The major reason was to create a practice that promises a peaceful and balanced life. Buddha did not preach it without any practice, he did walk the talk. He had first-hand experience in this approach before he started preaching it to his disciples and asked them to adhere to it. The take away here for the leaders is that they have to lead by example before they implement a plan, model, or any change. Leaders have to master their craft before asking others to follow, and this is the difference between a leader and a manager. Understanding and analysing one's environment increases the success rate of one's ability to direct his troops to execute a plan or idea.

**If you practice and gain spiritual energy, you will become as a spiritual leader, giving you the following six benefits which will drive you to success.**

**1. You will be able to help others make their own connection with the God they believe in**
A manager training his employee is similar to a spiritual leader training his disciples. While the

problem in hand may be different, the approach they should take up is the approach of enlightenment through questioning themselves and the process. This brings more clarity and makes understanding the process easy.

## 2. You will be able to lead others to find their own reason and identity

Workplace issues and strategic development becomes the tool to help followers discover their own personality and overcome obstacles standing in their way. By leading employees to function in areas in which they are strong will always be more productive than those who are simply trying to fill a position or role.

## 3. You will be able to transform others

A charismatic leader will be able to help their followers rediscover themselves, and help them redefine their priorities. This will pave way to loyalty, boosting morale, and higher efficiency on the job. Spiritual leadership will create passion within the followers and transform the powers within.

## 4. You can create an impact on the environment

When there is worry, fear, or indifference, a spiritual leader can transform the immediate power of these storms and restore vision, energy and hope. A spiritual leader can reduce the hostility of a situation and create a peaceful environment, he will be able to reduce hate and create love, can bring a sense of patience within his team members, treats everyone with kindness which will inspire his or her team morale, and works towards the greater goodness of the business as well as the individuals without cutting corners.

## 5. You can make people see old things with a different point of view

People have born and bred in a certain culture, and their thoughts dwell on the beliefs they were brought up with. Changing the way they think will do a lot of good in making business and life decisions, as they will be able to evaluate things from more than one view point.

## 6. You will gain followers because of who you are, not because of a position you hold

Leaders with spiritual beliefs give their employees more to think about and improvise on their own, rather than make them follow instructions. They lead by example, and followers start to follow them because they are inspired by their actions. A good example is Nelson Mandela, who is looked upon as a great leader by both Afrikaners as well as native blacks of South Africa.

## A HEALTHY LIFESTYLE

Healthy lifestyle is very important to keep your mind active and powerful, which is essential to your success.

# Six Steps to a Healthy Lifestyle

## 1. Healthy Eating
Maintain healthy eating habits and avoid eating fast food.

## 2. Maintaining Physical Fitness
Work out and try to maintain fitness through exercising. This lowers the risk of cholesterol and sugar levels.

## 3. Control Your Diet to avoid Blood Sugar
High blood sugar levels often are the leading cause of diabetes, and it has commonly resulted in blindness and other complications when treating other illnesses such as kidney diseases and nerve damage.

## 4. Control Your Diet to Maintain Healthy Blood Pressure Levels
Maintaining healthy blood pressure levels ensures that the body receives the needed blood at the correct speed and time. By maintaining a good green diet, the pressure levels are maintained.

## 5. Control Your Diet to Maintain Healthy Cholesterol Levels
It has been identified that high cholesterol levels have led to the hardening of arteries, which results in slow down of blood, and continuous ignorance will lead to permanent blockage, and hence, a heart attack.

## 6. Healthy Dieting

A lot of vegetables, fruits, and dairy products taken in a measured way enable us to be healthy. It was the correct mix of these natural products with herbs and spices that kept our ancestors living for a long period, before these so-called advanced medicines were created.

As mentioned in my earlier chapter, changes in the environment have been unpredictable, we have been hit by a recession, and markets have crashed, leading to a rise in unemployment rates. And it must be noted that certain businesses did thrive in this environment, which is an example why you must invest in yourself and empower yourself to be a force to be reckoned with. This book will act as a personal guide to help you assess *where you are now, where you want to get to or want to be, what the gap is, and how you can get there through perseverance and investing in yourself.* You deserve to have more of what you want out of life.

## CHAPTER 18

# LEARN FROM THE HISTORIES OF WORLD LEADERS

History is filled with the achievements of great leaders. By examining the past we can retain key attributes that will help us succeed to where we want to be.

*"There are so many people who have lived and died before you. You will never have a new problem; you're not going to ever have a new problem. Somebody wrote the answer down in a book somewhere."*

**– Will Smith**

So what were the great leaders so good at, and how did they achieve the things that made them great?

The short answer is that they weren't all good at everything, but quite the contrary. Each leader had their own strengths and weaknesses which drove them to where they are today, as an individual who's looked up upon by others as a great achiever. Many were so brilliant at certain things that it hid the fact that they were indifferent at others.

***When it comes to improving our skills, history's great leaders provide lessons for us. So learn from the leaders.***

As a leader, it is always very important to create a positive image about yourself amongst your key stakeholders, including employees, customers, your bank, etc. Learning to think like a confident leader doesn't come naturally. I am going to take the most successful leaders and explain what sort of leadership skills we can learn from them.

### <u>Henry Ford</u> (Ford Motor Company)

*"Failure is simply the opportunity to begin again, this time more intelligently. There is no disgrace in honest failure; there is disgrace in fearing to fail"*

Henry Ford can be said to be the inventor of assembly line, enabling companies to produce products in mass quantities. He produced the first of many American automobiles that was affordable to the majority of Americans. This assembly-line concept has spread to all mass consumer goods and fast foods, which we enjoy at low cost. He realized his vision of manufacturing an automobile for every American to afford.

Before, forming the company Ford Motor Company, Henry Ford worked as an apprentice machinist, and after that he became an engineer with the Edison Illuminating Company. He committed his awareness to personal experiments on gasoline engines. These experiments resulted in a self- driven vehicle which he called the Ford Quadricycle. Later, he formed the Ford Motor Company, and he built a car known as the Model T, which was cheap at the time. However, Ford needed to present a better motor vehicle. In 1927, successfully launched model A with better technical and engine design. This model sold more than 4 million units. One could say that the driving force for this innovation is captured by one of Henry Ford's sayings:

*"Enthusiasm is the yeast that makes your hopes shine to the stars. Enthusiasm is the sparkle in*

*your eyes, the swing in your gait. The grip of your hand, the irresistible surge of will and energy to execute your ideas."*

Henry Ford was one of the earliest free enterprise leaders to deduce that paying employees more was essential to retain talent and improve productivity and keep staff morale high. Even though he paid above market rates to employees he managed to manufacture affordable cars. This indicates a shrewd business leader who keeps all stakeholders happy.

His company is still one of the leading car manufacturers in the world.

**<u>Warren Buffett</u>** (The most successful investor of the 20th century)

*"I always knew I was going to be rich. I don't think I ever doubted it for a minute."*

Warren Buffett's path to success is indeed inspiring, hence it is certainly worthwhile learning a bit about this exemplary gentleman.

Warren Buffett is the primary shareholder, chairman, and CEO of Berkshire Hathaway Inc., which is an American multinational company that    oversees and manages a number of subsidiary companies.

Buffett was always an enthusiastic financier, even as a child he would work in several part time jobs in order to save up and invest in profitable ventures.

At the tender age of 11, Buffett bought his first stock, investing in 6 shares of Cities Service preferred stock. Over the years, Buffett invested wisely, allowing him to become a millionaire at the age of 32 and subsequently, in 1990, he became a billionaire.

Warren Buffett was determined to become a successful entrepreneur, thus it was his positive attitude which drove him into becoming the exemplary leader he is today.

In spite of Buffett's success, he leads a modest life in comparison to other successful entrepreneurs. He is an avid philanthropist who certainly believes in giving back.

It is his simplicity and determination that drove Warren Buffett to such a successful reign as one the world's most influential people.

**Six must-learn lessons from Warren Buffett to achieve success in your life.**

1. **On Earning**: "Never depend on single income. Make investment to create a second source."

   You should not depend on one income as this will take a long time to accumulate your wealth and also it will create fear inside you by thinking what will happen if you were to lose that income.

2. **On Spending**: "If you buy things you do not need, soon you will have to sell things you need."

   You have to have discipline. You have to buy only needed items, you should not waste any money on unwanted things.

3. **On Savings**: "Do not save what is left after spending, but spend what is left after saving."

   You have to prepare budget and spend your money. You have to put your savings first before any expenses. Not after.

4. **On Taking Risk**: "Never test the depth of the river with both the feet."

You should not use all of your resources. You have to be prepared for the worst case scenario of losing everything.

5. **On Investment**: "Do not put all your eggs in one basket."

You have to have a diversified portfolio. That means if you lose one investment, still you will be in the game. Putting all of your money in one type of investment is risky. For example, if you invest all of your money in gold and suddenly the gold price dropped, you will start worrying about your future. The ghost of fear will come into you.

6. **On Expectations**: "Honesty is a very expensive gift. Do not expect it from cheap people."

You have to be honest all the time. But you should not expect it from others. You have to take care of yourself all the time.

## Steve Jobs (Apple)

***"Sometimes life will hit you on the head with a brick, but don't lose faith."***

Steve Paul Jobs was one of the most prominent and well-known technological entrepreneurs of the modern century. Born on February 24, 1955, Steve was the brain behind the world-renowned company Apple, Inc., of which he was the co-founder, chairman and the CEO. Steve is well known as a creative genius who transformed the lives of many people around the world with the revolution of personal computing through Apple, Inc.

After a power struggle with the board, Steve was fired from his own company in 1985 and went on to establish NeXT. However, Jobs returned to Apple as an advisor years later and eventually became the CEO of the company. Steve brought Apple from near bankruptcy to profitability by 1998.

As the CEO of the company, Steve introduced the iMac, iTunes, iPod, iPhone, and iPad, which have revolutionized how people use mobile devices and computers in the modern era.

As an adopted child, Steve was always interested in electronics from a young age. Upon completing his high school graduation, Steve enrolled in Reed College, which proved to be an expensive college for his parents to afford.

After dropping out of college, Jobs frequently dropped in and out of creative classes such as calligraphy and slept on the floors of dorm rooms of his friends and returned used plastic bottles for cash. Jobs later said, "If I had never dropped in on that single calligraphy course in college, the Mac would have never had multiple typefaces or proportionally spaced fonts."

Steve was diagnosed with cancer in 2003 and underwent many treatments, including a liver transplant.

One of Steve's most inspiring quotes is *"Your time is limited, so don't waste it living someone else's life. Don't be trapped by dogma - which is living with the results of other people's thinking. Don't let the noise of others' opinions drown out your own inner voice and most importantly have the courage to follow your heart and intuition."* Steve always encouraged living life based on what makes you happy and not living the lives other people want you to have.

With his never-ending thirst for seeking what he loves to do in life Steve has always been one of the most inspiring people in the modern era.

## <u>Richard Branson</u> (Virgin)

*"Never be afraid of weakness, always find a way to convert your weakness into your strength. Experiment with your life and enjoy it to the fullest. Create new paths for your future generations. Screw it, let's do it."*

Are leaders made or born? This is an age-old question, one which remains debatable. Whatever makes an individual rise above the rest and set a whole new standard is what gets us all interested in seeking knowledge about such people, in order to determine what inspired them in becoming extraordinary.

Richard Branson is one such individual, who rose above the rest and is still going strong, not only as a successful businessman, but also as a dedicated philanthropist. He is the founder and chairman of Virgin Group.

*Losing my Virginity* is one of the first autobiographies I read about an exceptional person and one of the books I have always insisted my loved ones should set their eyes upon.

Branson dropped out of school at the age of sixteen; he had a poor academic record as he struggled with dyslexia (Developmental Reading Disorder (DRD)). Being dyslexic never was Branson's downfall; in fact, this was his motivation for becoming the charismatic leader he is today.

Whilst launching campaigns for his many companies, Branson made sure his marketing material would pass on the message the very first time it was launched. This was because being dyslexic guided him in the way he communicated with his customers. Therefore, if he understood the message the first time round and perceived it to be noteworthy, he would go ahead with such marketing material for his campaigns. This attribute, together with confidence, persistence and determination, made him a successful entrepreneur.

As observers and critics, we could certainly agree that what drove Richard Branson to success was his weakness, as he took his weakness and made it his strength, and the rest is history!

## **Bill Gates** (Microsoft)

*"As we look ahead into the next century, leaders will be those who empower others."*

William Henry "Bill" Gates is yet another prominent and well-known technological entrepreneur of the modern century. Born on October 28, 1955, Bill was the co-founder, chairman and the CEO of Microsoft.

Bill Gates is constantly ranked amongst the richest people in the world and has been in the higher ranks for almost two decades.

At the age of 13, Bill enrolled in the Lakeside School where he got the chance to write his first computer program, an application of tic-tac-toe where the user could play games against the computer.

Bill graduated Lakeside School in 1973 and enrolled in Harvard College from which he later dropped out to form a software company along with Paul Allen.

This was the beginning of Microsoft.

During his tenure at Microsoft, Bill broadened the company with a range of many products, helping develop the personal computer revolution.

Bill also encourages pursuing life based on what a person loves to do. He also strongly believes in learning from your mistakes. One of his quotes – *"It's fine to celebrate success, but it is more important to heed the lessons of failure"* – emphasizes learning from your failures and mistakes to become a better person.

Bill is a strong believer of books being important to developing his vision and helping him dream and pursue what he loves to do. He said, *"I really had a lot of dreams when I was a kid, and I think a great deal of that grew out of the fact that I had a chance to read a lot."*

Bill Gates is a strong believer in philanthropy. He believes in giving back and has signed up to donate the majority of his wealth to charity. Bill Gates has been an inspiring person to many people, especially with his contributions in the information technology arena.

## Mark Zuckerberg (Facebook)

*"I believe that over time, people get remembered for what they build, and if you build something great, people don't care about what someone says about you in a movie... they care about what you build."*

Facebook is one of the popular household names in the current era. And the man behind this name is Mark Zuckerbeg, who was born in May 14, 1984 and is one of the co-founders, chairman and CEO of Facebook. Mark is recognized as an Internet Entrepreneur as well as an avid philanthropist who has signed up to donate most of his wealth to charity.

Mark launched Facebook from his dorm room in college, and by 2012, he was considered to be a prodigy in computer programming, something he had showed keen interest in since a young age. After enrolling into Harvard, Mark developed Facebook as a networking tool amongst local colleges and then later took it on to other campuses and countrywide.

Mark eventually dropped out of Harvard to continue his project and now is regarded as one of the 100 wealthiest and most influential people in the world by *Time* magazine.

Mark emphasizes finding what you are passionate about and pursuing it. In the following quote, Mark describes on his passions and how they drove him to be who he is today:

*"Find that thing you are super passionate about. A lot of founding principles of Facebook are that if people have access to more information and are more connected, it will make the world better; people will have more understanding, more empathy. That's the guiding principle for me. On hard days, I really just step back, and that's the thing that keeps me going."*

Mark is an inspiration to many of the younger generation with his passionate approach on pursuing what he loves. Beginning as a young computer programmer, Mark has emerged as one of the most successful people below 30 years of age.

Based on the above studies, it is very clear that to become a successful person first of all you should have the passion to achieve your goal. Being an entrepreneur or leader is not an easy task. It involves developing more people and delegating the tasks to achieve your goals. In the meantime, you have to keep your stakeholders happy.

When you become a leader, success is all about developing your followers. It's about making the people who work for you smarter, bigger and bolder. Nothing you do anymore as an individual matters except supporting your team members to achieve your goals as a team.

Following your passion, converting your weaknesses into strengths, enjoying your life, and delegation is the art of leadership.

## CHAPTER 19

# THE POWERFUL FORMULA FOR SUCCESS

**DREAM -> VISION -> GOAL => SUCCESS**

**THE POWER OF DREAMS**

*"If you can dream it, you can do it."*
— **Walt Disney**

<u>Dreams</u> *will create burning desires*

Whatever you can dream of, you can achieve. But you have to put in the effort needed to make them work. What do you want more than anything in the world?

Stop right now and write down your answer.

If you don't know the answer, close your eyes and take time to find the answer. What make you happy? Why?

*"All our dreams can come true, if we have the courage to pursue them."*
— **Walt Disney**

You have to prioritise your dreams. Decide on which one is most important to you and focus purely on that. Always take things one step at a time. Make sure you are clear on what you intend to gain from that particular dream of yours, is it success, self-satisfaction or fame. For some of you it may be a combination of all three. You have to write down the reasons why your dreams are important, the *"whys"* that will give you the purpose, passion and power of life. It will wake you up early in the morning and keep you up late at night. When you know the reasons why you are doing it, you will have a burning desire that will drive you to go the extra mile.

**Walt Disney**

The creator of the international cultural icon

134

Mickey Mouse, Walt Disney started the Disney Empire with great determination and guts. At the age of 22, Walt went into bankruptcy after the failure of a cartoon series. He went to Los Angeles with $40 in cash and a few clothes. Walt and his brother then set up a nascent animation business in California.

Inexperienced in business, Walt had to face problems of the ownership of his animated characters. He realized that the ownership of the animated cartoon character Oswald the Lucky was with the distributor. The power the distributor had over Walt and his other artists eventually led him to relinquish the business and start one on his own again.

Walt Disney was once quoted as saying, *"As long as there is imagination left in the world, Disneyland will never be complete."* Although Disney theme parks were not yet built at the time, Walt Disney's imagination led him to start another character, Mickey Mouse, with his old and loyal friend. This iconic Mickey Mouse character had many infectious and enjoyable traits such as his energetic and enjoyable personality, entertaining actions and most important of all, laughter.

Walt Disney said that *"Laughter is America's most important export."* Walt Disney identified that he needed to create new character to satisfy a growing nation's appetite for humour.

Today, after his death, the Disney Empire is still going strong.

## THE POWER OF VISION

You have to have the vision to drive yourself quickly towards success. You have to visualise every single day that you have already reached that level and enjoy that feeling. This will power your mind and will create the burning desire towards success.

*"If you are working on something exciting that you really care about, you don't have to be pushed. The vision pulls you."*

**– Steve Jobs**

### Learn the power of VISION from Abraham Lincoln

Abraham Lincoln's VISIONARY leadership abolished slavery in the United States. Abraham Lincoln was the 16th president of the United States of America, as which he served from March 1861 until his assassination in April 1865. His determination to end slavery was finally recognized in 1865 by which salves were freed in nationwide.

Being regarded as one of the Americas greatest

heroes, Lincoln possessed a unique appeal which had an incredible impact on the nation; he used such traits to bring about the best in the United States.

His rise to being the 16th president of the United States was from a humble beginning. His beloved mother died at the age of 34 when Abraham was just 9 years old, this alienated him from his father even more with whom he did not bond well. His father remarried, but unlike typical step mothers Sarah bonded well with Abraham, it was she who encouraged Abraham to read. Abraham received his formal education whilst growing into his manhood, an estimation of 18 months in total. He was mostly self-educated; in fact, he educated himself in becoming a successful lawyer.

His political career began in 1832 by which he ran for a seat in the Illinois House of Representatives, but he lost the election. He ran again in 1834, and won; he served in the Illinois House of Representatives until 1842.

Abraham Lincoln was elected president on 6th November 1860 and assumed office on 4th March 1861. He was re-elected on 8th November 1864 and served until his assassination on 15th April 1865.

Lincoln was a determined man not only to succeed for himself but also for the country he loved so much.

*"Always bear in mind that your own resolution to succeed is more important than any one thing."*

- **Abraham Lincoln**

## THE POWER OF GOALS

"Goals are Dreams with a Deadline." In other words, it's fine to dream of owning an island in the Pacific Ocean but what are your chances of ever actually doing it? Dreaming is fun, but goal setting is actually serious business.

Your goals must be realistic, and something you truly believe you can achieve. Your goals must have a deadline by when you want to reach them. Your goals also should be specific with measurable targets. Instead of saying, *"I want to be financially secure,"* specify what you actually want: *"I will sell 50 toys by Christmas."*

For example, if you're an architect constructing an apartment, you would have specific tasks to complete by a certain date. You would complete one step and then move on to the next, with the end goal of finishing the entire building by a certain date. You would dig out the hole for the foundation, and then you would pour the foundation. You would build the frame, and then continue each necessary task until your building is complete. So the main fact to take in is that you should use small goals as a blueprint to achieve your larger goal.

*"If you want to live a happy life, tie it to a goal, not to people or things."*
**– Albert Einstein**

Determine what steps you'll have to take to achieve your goals. For example, you're a small business trying to expand by selling a brand new innovative product. The first steps you would take is to do your market research and see whether it would be cost effective.

Write down your goals! Don't keep them in your head! Once you've written them down, share them with your partner, your best friend, or a colleague. Sharing them will help you feel responsible, and you will have the desire and willpower to work harder to reach your goals. You have to remember that your goals are not written in stone. You have to set goals to start. As time passes and you gain more experience and learn more about your business, you can always modify your goals, mainly your long-term ones.

In order to accomplish your goals, you may have

to acquire some new skills and step out of your comfort zone. You must be willing to do whatever it takes! Change is not something you should be afraid of; it's the one thing that you should face head on.

**"You can only become truly accomplished at something you love. Don't make money your goal. Instead, pursue the things you love doing, and then do them so well that people can't take their eyes off you."**

**– Maya Angelou**

*Never give up! If you are determined to succeed, and if you KNOW that you can, nothing can stop you!*

Setting goals and achieving them is a vital part of success. But this is not a goal setting book, so I can't go into more detail on how to set or achieve goals.

However, my mentor and friend Raymond Aaron has written a best-selling hardcover book, *Double Your Income Doing What You Love*. Raymond is recognised as the world's # 1 authority on goal achievement.

In fact, on the back cover, there are testimonials from giant celebrities who use his program. One such testimonial is by Jack Canfield, the co-creator of the *Chicken Soup For The Soul* series of books.

Here is his testimonial: *"The reason I personally chose to use this amazing system for myself and for my company is that, bluntly stated, it is the most powerful system ever created."*

By special arrangement, I have permission to allow you, my dear reader, to own a copy of Mr. Aaron's book for free and you can get it by instant download simply by going to his website. www.aaron.com.

## CHAPTER 20

# HOW TO OVERCOME PROCRASTINATION

*"Procrastination is the bad habit of putting off until the day after tomorrow what should have been done the day before yesterday."*

- Napoleon Hill

Procrastination permits your mind and body to switch off from being productive. Procrastination will reduce your self-esteem and also will lower your reputation in the eyes of others. This needs to be solved with immediate effect by making sure you take necessary action.

**Six Action Plan Guides to Overcoming Procrastination:**

**1. Just start!**

You have to start first. No point in talking. You have to take action now. If you are planning to start a business, start today! Start now! Once you have started a task, you will feel great about yourself, which will drive you forward towards success. You have to create a to-do list and organise your time to get your entire task done as per your schedule.

Once you gain momentum, you will become more productive and thus beating the battle against procrastination.

## 2. Take Breaks and Think about the Next Step

This will help you immensely to eliminate procrastination. Taking short breaks, for just, say, 15 minutes after working for a solid period of time, will refresh your thoughts and prevent your mind from wandering. You could take short refreshing breaks, do some light exercise, practice some breathing techniques, or even meditation will allow you to work more efficiently and to stay more productive to finish your task rather than procrastinating. However, technological distractions should be minimised for your short breaks to be effective.

## 3. Be Motivated

You should always list the most important tasks first on your list to try and avoid temptation of leaving them till the last minute. By ticking of the most important tasks first will give you self-accomplishment and motivation. This motivation will give you the willingness to complete the rest of the minor things pending on your list.

## 4. Keep Commitments Under Control

You should try and avoid committing to too many things. Prioritise your time enabling you to have some time for relaxation for both your mind and body. By keeping your commitments under control you are less likely to procrastinate as there will be fewer tasks to focus on and people will take less advantage you by piling on more and more work for you to do, thinking that you will be able to cope.

## 5. Delegate Your Tasks

You have to learn to delegate your task to the right people and provide clear instructions and guidance for them. You have to give clear instructions during the delegation and also monitor the progress. This will help you to reach long term success.

This will allow you with some extra time to concentrate on key tasks and also to focus on how to drive your business forward.

## 6. Improve Your Decision Making and Time Management Skills.

If you want to get your task done, either you have to have the sound time management skills to finish all tasks on time or you have to take the decision to delegate it to someone to get that job done. Therefore, both decision making skills and time management skills are essential to overcoming procrastination.

Chapter 21

# HOW TO TURN DEFEAT INTO VICTORY

Defeat, most of us are afraid to face. Sometimes we don't try anything new mainly due to fear of failure. Fear of failure is one of greatest negative factors which can make a person think that he cannot do anything in his life. I have a friend who was a very intelligent chap in our school. After leaving school, he was the first person to get a job in a leading firm. We were really proud of him. Life moved on, and after three years I met him. I asked him how he was. He replied, *"Horrible, man."* He continued, *"I am unable to complete my undergraduate degree. I cannot study. I have failed so many times. Now I quit my job also. I'm not*

147

*going anywhere."* I asked him how he was financing himself. He replied in a low voice, *"My mother is providing for me again."*

It is always important to stay focused during the hard times. Everyone fails in their life. It is all about how you fight back.

*"I never thought of losing, but now that it's happened, the only thing is to do it right. That's my obligation to all the people who believe in me. We all have to take defeats in life."*

**–Muhammad Ali**

Ali was a normal African American guy who, by realizing his gift of speed, achieved great success. He never feared any of the obstacles that came his way in the form of racism, and became stronger in spirit with every problem faced in his life.

Ali became heavyweight champion of the world after beating Sunny Liston in 1964.

At the peak of his boxing career Ali had to face the Vietnam War draft, and Ali refused to go. Due to this, Ali was stripped of his boxing title and license and could not fight for nearly two years.

After his return in 1970, Ali, still undefeated, had to face all-conquering Joe Frazier, also known as "Smoking Joe." The bout went on for 15 bloody and gruesome rounds and Joe Frazier was declared the winner. Ali was in his early thirties and had difficulty facing superior punching and speed of younger boxers. However, Ali was asked to fight recently-crowned heavyweight champion George Foreman, who had convincingly beat Joe Frazier to regain the title. All the people were in favor of George Foreman; they said he could beat Ali with ease.

However, Muhammad Ali adopted a successful strategy, the "Rope-A-Dope," where he made his opponent throw punches while Ali leaned on the ropes. George foreman's punches rarely hit Ali. This method made George Foreman expend all his energy and tire. Ali then sensed his time to retaliate and sent down a flurry of punches to knock down the unconquerable and superior George Foreman.

This proves why Ali is still considered the greatest, because he had to fight the best of the best in his era. It's not about losing; it's all about how you come back.

## Six Steps to Turn Defeat into Victory

1. **Study your own failure to overcome failure** - There is a famous quote by Thomas A. Edison: ***"I have not failed. I've just found 10,000 ways that won't work."*** It is a fact that so many people fail miserably and give up their passion very easily with the first defeat. It is all about you identifying the reason for your failure and developing strategies to overcome those temporary defeats.

2. **Have the courage to be your own constructive critic** – You cannot find a better friend than yourself. If we look at the most successful people, they know their weaknesses. For example if we take Sir Alan Sugar, he said, *"I am gambler. I take high risks. Sometimes I get high rewards, sometimes I fail miserably."* So he consults with his high calibre, top-level management before investing in risky projects. However, the final decision is made by Sir Alan Sugar.

3. **Believe in your ideas** – It's really useful to get other peoples' opinions about your failures. The answer can provide a different perspective. However, it is very important that you believe in your ideas and also make sure third parties' negative feedback doesn't sink you very deeply into failure.

4. **Stop blaming luck**
   You have to study each of your defeats to find out what went wrong, how it went wrong, and why it went wrong to prevent repetition in the future by taking necessary steps immediately. You have to remember that blaming luck never got anyone where they wanted to go.

5. **Blend persistence with experimentation**
   You have to be very proactive and think about the outcome well in advance. Stay with your goal; try new approaches and experiment.

## 6. *See the good side*

You have to remember that there is a good side to every situation. You have to find it, see the good side, and overcome discouragement.

## CHAPTER 22

# THINK BIG AND THINK POSITIVE

It is a true fact that when you are thinking positively you will feel relaxed and more energetic. No long-term success is possible without a positive attitude. This will enable us to develop action plans to achieve our dreams.

One of greatest examples for positive thinking is Michael Jordan, an American former professional basketball player and entrepreneur. MJ was born on February 17, 1963 and is recognized by many people around the world. The National Basketball Association (NBA) website praises MJ as *"By acclamation, the greatest basketball player of all time."*

Michael's **strong determination, rigorous training** and his **attitude** saw him excel in the professional arena where he won many awards and recognitions, such as the most valuable player for five times, and he went on to become a fan favourite. Michael also made impressive comebacks after injuries which at times kept him out of play for months in a row.

Michael also represented his country in the Olympics twice, and in his first Olympic games, he was still a college player.

*"I play to win, whether during practice or a real game. And I will not let anything get in the way of me and my competitive enthusiasm to win."*

This quote by Michael Jordan shows his passion and commitment to winning.

Michael also emphasizes how a failure needs to be capitalized and learnt from and turned into success. This famous quote by him has inspired many people around the world. *"I've missed more than 9000 shots in my career. I've lost almost 300 games. 26 times, I've been trusted to take the game winning shot and missed. I've failed over and over and over again in my life. And that is why I succeed."*

*"Some people want it to happen, some wish it would happen, others make it happen."*
— **Michael Jordan**

How to build positive thinking, a **Six-step** guide:

1. **Understand that you create your own destiny** – It is always very important for you to understand that you create your own destiny. So it is your responsibility to create your path to success. There are so many people in this world that, when they fail, they put the burden on other people and don't do anything to overcome their failure. You don't want to be one of them. Always have a tight grip on your life. Don't let others control your life.

2. **Make a strong commitment to think positively and not to think negatively** – You can develop these skills by reading books and by reading about successful people and watching motivational videos, etc. Continuous training and development will enable your mind to think positively even when you are failing.

3. **Be grateful for what you have today** – It is always very important to accept the fact there are so many people in this world having a poorer lifestyle than you. Some people are being treated like slaves and not given any human rights. So utilize your time in an effective way; don't spoil it by thinking

negatively. We all are going to be here only once, so make it worthwhile.

4. **Avoid everything that can negatively influence your thinking** – The environment you live in is one of great factors that influence your thinking patterns. There will be people who will always give negative feedback to your approach. It is also a true fact that so many people are so afraid that they don't try to do anything new in their life and are content with living a mediocre lifestyle.

5. **Try humor** – It can be a difficult task to keep a positive attitude when there is little hope for success. No matter how hard life hits you back, it is very important to keep your humor. It will help you to reduce stress and boost your outlook.

6. **Try not to worry; enjoy your life** – There is a strong negative relationship between negative thinking and confidence level. So if we keep on worrying, it is not going to add any value to our life. The only consequence is we may end up making an appointment with the doctor. Trying not to worry is an art. When you realize that your life is limited, you will start to live your life to its fullest.

*You have to surround yourself with highly motivated people and winners. Under any circumstances, you should not allow any negative people to bring you down. You have to find the way to do better and add value to other people and yourself.*

## CHAPTER 23

# MANAGE YOUR TIME

Time is more important than Money

*"Time is our most valuable asset, yet we tend to waste it, kill it, and spend it rather than invest it."*

— Jim Rohn

Most people leave home at 8 am for work and come back at 6 pm, then dinner, TV, Facebook and so on. So you do not have the time to think of something else which could bring more fortune in the future. This has to be changed. You have to prioritise your tasks and keep yourself free to develop yourself towards success. You have to invest your time to learn new skills, try new opportunities and inspire others.

As is always said, *"time is precious"*; it's something that cannot be retrieved, so make the most of it.

**Six Steps Guide to Improve Your Time Management Skills**

1. Make a list
2. Prioritise and do the important task first
3. Reward yourself for accomplishment of a task
4. Focus on one thing at a time
5. Avoid procrastination
6. Set a deadline and monitor your progress

## <u>Opportunities</u>

You have to be an open-minded person to spot opportunities around you.

*"If there is a God, he is within. You don't ask God to give you things; you depend on God for your inner theme."*

– **Bruce Lee**

**A story of opportunities:**

In a small village lived a man who spent his entire life serving God. One day heavy rain and flooding started. The whole village was filled with water which was slowly deepening. That man stayed in his place and prayed to God to save him. A boat went by with lots of people on board. A woman cried out to the man to come aboard, however, the man replied that the God which he prayed to would save him. Finally as the water deepened up to his shoulders, a log floated by for him to hold on to and survive, however, he was determined that his God would save him. Eventually he drowned. When he reached heaven, he asked God, "I served my entire life for you, why did you not save me?" God then replied, "I did, my son. I gave you so many opportunities. I was the one on the boat who cried for you to come aboard and I was the floating log urging you to grab hold. It was you who missed all those opportunities given to you and now you blame me for your mistakes."

*"To hell with circumstances; I create opportunities."*

**– Bruce Lee**

Now what the story is merely telling us is that you create your own opportunities; don't rely on others to get you there.

## Persistence with Patience

Persistence is the ability to stick with something. The majority of people face failure because of their lack of persistence in creating alternative plans to take the place of those which fail.

*"Patience, persistence and perspiration make an unbeatable combination for success"*

**– Napoleon Hill**

## Six Steps guide to improve your Persistence

1. You have to write down your purpose
2. You have to create a burning desire within yourself
3. You have to create will power
4. You have to stop acting on guesses
5. You have to gain accurate knowledge
6. You have to overcome all of your fears

## TREAT YOURSELF LIKE A KING

You are the most valuable asset. Treat yourself like a king and always think that you are the most important and powerful person on the planet. You are the only one person who can control yourself.

Made in the USA
Middletown, DE
25 June 2017